pisces

february 20 • march 20

vmb
PUBLISHERS

contents

Text by
Patrizia Troni

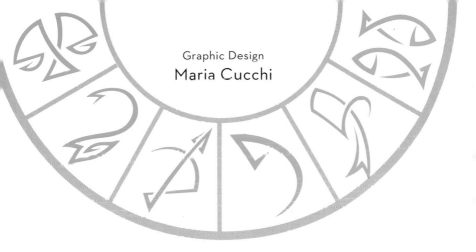

Graphic Design
Maria Cucchi

Character and Temperament

Pisces is the last sign of the Zodiac, the one that has always closed off the circle. Pisces symbolizes the transition from one cycle that has exhausted its drive (and thus already belongs to the past) and another that is starting, giving rise to rebirth and renewal, a new form.

Pisces is compatible with an enlarged consciousness, with an awareness that what is about to end is also that which is beginning. Pisces is the sign of that which precedes the beginning, birth, corresponding to what comes before space, time and light. Therefore, Pisces is in immediate contact with what could be called the divine, the otherworldly, thus posing the great question concerning the existence that we all have in common. That place outside of space and time is infinity, and Pisces has a particular sensitivity, a profound spirituality that connects with the infinite. So, while the last sign of the Zodiac symbolizes the end of a cycle, it also heralds something that is rising, life itself. Thus, Pisces is everything that prepares, plans, expects, awaits, and firmly believes in, what is to come, almost defeating the ineluctability of death.

This means that on an individual level Pisces is the most magical personality in the Zodiac. Pisces does not live with and abide by the cold and rigorous precepts of rationality and logic, but grasp the essence of things through uncommon insight and extraordinary sensitivity. Pisces has a fantastic heart, but unlike the other Water signs, which are equally sensitive and insightful, never wants to be enclosed and suffocated by limits and the restrictions of precise and definite identity.

Pisces is the sign of chaos, in the sense that their antennae are synchronized with everything, and even though details do not escape their notice, it is the sense of the absolute that characterizes them, unfolding and revealing areas of the spirit and the universe to them.

Their magical sensitivity always wants to go further; it wants to explore what lies beyond the confines through endless movement that is the transformation of identity, change, evolution, with an idea in their heart that can also become cosmic compassion.

Those they meet with for the first time or whom they already know understand that, with Pisces, one goes beyond the limits and narrow confines of rules and conventions. Because Pisces has a wider perspective and their heart, which follows the visionary light of intuition, always pursues a great idea, although, at the moment, this might not appear to be the ultimate in realism or pragmatism. True, everyday life demands that one keeps their feet firmly on the ground, accept certain habits, and follow stable and repetitive practices. But, Pisces never abandons their visions and dreams, which often correspond to a desire to change the world.

Others say they are strange, different, often distracted, with their head in the clouds, almost absent, one could say. In reality, this vague, bizarre, confused and exaggerated behavior soon proves to be an intangible spiritual asset with respect to the material world, which is sometimes so sterile and brutal.

Airy, light, elusive, able to appear and disappear suddenly, with a delicate spirit that vibrates without exaggeration, Pisces represents, in the grand context of the Zodiac, the domain of a pulsating, passionate heart that, with its magic, seeks a harmonious bond with the world which, all too often, is rejected in our Western society.

Love and Passion

8 Pisces

For Pisces, love is a marvelous thing, and while it may sometimes entail suffering and torment, this only makes it more beautiful and worthy of being experienced to the greatest extent. Their love is cosmic, open, dynamic, never the same; it is love based on sudden storms, waves that rise up to the sky, overwhelming emotions and sensations, and remarkable, inexhaustible imagination.

Love is never habit, lifeless assurance and security, which slips into the quagmire of comfort and boredom, but is something that emerges from the subconscious, like an ocean that has alternating moments of absolute calm and storms that are impossible to withstand. Love for Pisces must be amazement, apparition, vision and, above all, magic. It is enveloped in poetic feeling and communicates through extrasensory perception. The sensitivity of their heart, like that of their psyche, is enormous and becomes the triumph of the senses, powerful and overwhelming sensuality that is, at the same time, always delicate.

Love is never gross, vulgar, or connected to anything purely materialistic or opportunistic. Rather, it is sweetness, and tenderness, as well as escape. Above all, it must be surprise, including whatever deviates from the norm and allows Pisces to explore territory with an enchanting atmosphere. True, Pisces is then able to introduce sentiment and affection into everyday life, putting all they have into a concrete project and policy of living as a couple. Yet for them, love must never lose sight of that magic and poetry whose power their big heart feeds on. Consequently, they can be sentimental, romantic, enamored of love, able to be captivated by many different feelings and sensations in the same day.

Pisces always needs affection and is always tender, sweet, and at times fragile, but with very intense feeling that relishes those microscopic and invisible sensations that enhance their exaggerated power of perception. They like to seduce, conquer, dream, suggest, suspend, leave and resume, at times even with a certain apprehension, with tremors that become grace and delicious delicacy. Sometimes timid and at other times audacious, their love goes beyond the narrow confines of egoistic needs. Besides being overpowering passion, it also consists of compassion, understanding and helpfulness, bringing comfort and support to all those who suffer. They seduce and conquer without being aggressive and usually with a discreet and moderate style made up of whispered words that slowly and progressively crumble even the hardest rocks.

Often, they enjoy combining affection and feeling with a spirit of sacrifice, with their capacity to devote themselves entirely to others, with the pleasure of losing themselves in, and becoming everything for, others.

They like the vibration of love when it becomes a quivering thrill. They adore thinking about love all day long, and some of them are even capable of sheer folly in order to pursue that vibration. But passion, however intense and all-embracing it may be, however much it wants to transcend all barriers and limits and merge the body and heart in a single expression, cannot become stable, fixed like a square building that will never change. This is because love, for them, is continuous transformation, an understanding with their partner that combines deep affection with the most audacious fantasy, including special erotic experiences.

Like no other sign, they know how to enjoy the pleasures of the flesh by stimulating it with their inexhaustible imagination, and they also know how to combine affection and sexual desire more than the other signs, because pleasure, for them, is not a merely a materialistic approach, since it is tripled in intensity and value with the richness of the spirit.

How to Hook a Pisces and How to Let Them Go

Just as Antoine de Saint-Exupéry wrote in *The Little Prince*, "It is only with the heart that one *can see* rightly; what is essential is invisible to the eye." Pisces understands with the heart, speaks with the heart and decides with the heart. It takes only a moment for them to fall in love, a moment to escape, a moment to decide that someone is the right person or to lose their head and leave that person for another. This does not mean that they are unreliable, merely that they have an oceanic need for love, that they are ready for sacrifice and total devotion, but that, if they are not treated in the same way, they start looking for a new romantic relationship.

The female Pisces is a very sweet and astute geisha who knows how to treat her man – much less fragile and defenseless than she sometimes appear to be. In order to be in harmony, a bouquet of flowers, accompanied by some sweet nothing, will touch her sentimental side. Another efficacious move is to take a romantic walk, bearing in mind that the female Pisces is certainly sentimental, but she also has a fluid side that demands room and must not be suffocated by pressing requests or habitual rhythms. The male Pisces often conceals his delicate nature behind a mask of virile coolness, but he is really a softhearted person who plunges into love. He is attracted by sweet, unpredictable, feminine women, women with whom he can freely express his fantasy (which is quite lively even from an erotic standpoint) and who understand when they must be there for him and when they should disappear. For those born under Pisces love is eternal, so it is by no means easy to break a relationship with them. If you want to leave Pisces, remember that they tend to be melodramatic: their threats, sobs, and desperation must not alarm you too much. Tearful apologies and touching words about the love that is coming to an end can sweeten the break, together with the promise that you will see each other again soon and you will never completely end the relationship.

Compatibility with Other Signs

The Zodiac signs that are most compatible with Pisces are Cancer, Taurus, Capricorn and Scorpio. Cancer puts Pisces in the center of their world and vice versa. This might create a secluded couple that tends to live in its own magic circle and shuts itself off from the outside world. With Cancer, Pisces attains the sublime height of passion as well as depths of pathos that make the relationship more stimulating.

The serene, practical, concrete Taurus is very good for Pisces, which is at times a bit apprehensive and restless. While on an erotic plane they have a fine relationship with a Taurus partner, with Scorpio it becomes stratospheric, since the bond with them is marked by magnetic attraction and thrilling sex. With Capricorn, they seem to have few things in common: they are tender and Capricorn is tough, they are flexible and Capricorn is rigid. But the attraction exists all the same, because if Capricorn territory is inundated with Pisces water then the result is deep feeling made up of respect, comprehension, support and unconditional affection.

Theoretically, relations with Virgo and Sagittarius are not very smooth. The former are attentive to every detail, parsimonious and rigorous, while Pisces is light years away from regulations and limits. Sagittarius has a big heart, but their overwhelming energy clashes with your need for moments of withdrawal and solitude. Other signs with which the art of compromise is essential are Aquarius, Libra and Gemini: they flow in Air while you do so in Water, thus, finding the middle ground is difficult, but not impossible. You get along with Aries and Leo as long as their blunt, imperious character does not offend your susceptibilities.

Lastly, friendship, love and total agreement are readily established with others born under Pisces. However, in a couple, it is important that at least one have their feet firmly on the ground.

Pisces Profession and Career

If Pisces manages to restrain their emotional side – which often jumbles too many ideas, projects and objectives – and be more constant, methodical, concrete and rational, they can be truly outstanding in their line of work. In fact, they have two rather rare qualities: their ingenuity, which immediately finds the solution and the right course of action to follow, and their sensitive heart, which allows them to understand others – colleagues, clients, collaborators, superiors, subordinates and employees – and create a truly harmonious communicative atmosphere in the workplace. This is because they take their sentimental and marvelously empathetic spirit there as well, thus succeeding in bringing to light the hidden and creative resources of a work group. When they are heading a team, it is that almost magical collaborative atmosphere that brings about the attainment of very important results, which are sometimes also surprising and exceptionally innovative. If, on the other hand, the harmony and like-mindedness of the heart are lacking and the work becomes dull routine based merely on their sense of duty, then they become depressed and lose the enthusiasm indispensable for doing their utmost.

If we must find fault with their character, it is their indecision, the vacillation that sometimes triggers those contradictions in which they think one thing and then do another, or the distraction that causes them to make hasty mistakes that could have easily been avoided.

Certainly, most of them need a job based on receptiveness, vital space and dynamism and that might entail traveling, novelty and surprises that intensify the spirit of adventure and search that characterizes them. Assembly lines, and being cooped up in an office with no prospects, where they spend hours with the usual documents or papers, are not for them. Should they have this type of job then their mind will readily go off at a tangent and fantasize instead of being concrete and concentrating on the boring work on their desk.

They must always pursue a dream, even in the workplace. They make excellent entrepreneurs (setting up a business and being self-employed are enterprises associated with Pisces) because they are idealists, they like utopias, the construction of something that stems from their mind and vision and that they cultivate as their personal product.

Every so often, they suffer from changes of mood, moments of disorientation with isolated let-ups that are more due to moodiness than substantial problems. When faced with complications they seem to be lost, but in reality, it is in moments of difficulty that they are at their best and find, in their rich subconscious, unexpected answers and solutions that flabbergast everybody. As in their private life, in the workplace they experience strange forms of fear, but their great sensitivity, which on the one hand might be a limit at times, on the other is an exceptional gift that they are able to make use of in the best possible way.

Empathetic, sociable, delicate and well liked in general by those close to them, they compensate for a rather limited practical sense with their imagination and inventiveness. They embody genius and intemperance, but in a solid context and with a stable base. A spirit like theirs could be an indispensable asset in the company for whom they work.

Since bringing comfort and aid is a typical feature of Pisces, many of them are physicians, nurses, nuns, social workers and volunteers who help others in need, while many others are entrepreneurs, are engaged in work connected to water – sailors, skippers, fishermen, divers and firemen – and are also excellent economists, musicians, fashion and graphic designers, authors and people engaged in activities connected to religion and spirituality. The correspondence Pisces has with enclosed places also connects them to prisons, convents and colleges.

❄ ❄ ❄ ❄ ❄ ❄ ❄

How Pisces Thinks and Reasons

Pisces is the sign of chaos, and vagueness, and because of their proverbial distraction, they are often the object of irony on the part of those who know them. Yet this lack of cold rationality and symmetrical logic stems from their greatest quality, their extraordinary capacity to perceive things, together with a sensitivity that makes them see everything, sometimes too much, almost with a proclivity to perceive the invisible in a very delicate and subtle, yet incontrovertible, way.

Their intelligence does not view things one at a time, in a rather monotonous and boring, overly reliable order, but rather seems to be overwhelmed by an ocean of emotions, as if they felt everything at once in an instant, at one blow. It is the subconscious of their most profound and inaccessible spirit that allows them to grasp truth that is denied to others. Their intuition goes straight to the essence of things; therefore, while it is true that they are sometimes somewhat distracted and irrational, when it comes to understanding the heart of a matter they do so before everyone else.

More than understanding, they feel; more than reasoning, they grasp immediately; more than reflecting, they find the solution a moment before even beginning to think about it.

If they should ever manage to let themselves be guided by instinct and rationally elaborate what their imagination has given them a glimpse of, they would be invincible. At times, they make the mistake of not believing in themselves totally, partly because it is not easy for them to express their remarkable instinct, but they should trust their perceptive antennae more.

Their intimacy with their subconscious is translated into creativity, imagination and the capacity to understand others, not so much because of their outward behavior or what they say, as for what they have in their hearts. Their sensitive and compassionate soul understands through their heart, and should some details escape their notice it is because they go right to the essence of things. They are enchanted not so much by the form as by the content that lies behind the form.

Naturally, this does not mean that they are not able to deal with everyday life, for many born under Pisces have attained very prestigious positions and there are crucial moments when they demonstrate that they are more practical and concrete than others. They are the primordial Water sign, the Great Ocean that contains everything, thus, they are able to transcend the minor datum or detail that intelligent and

rational people often end up dwelling on to no purpose. Their visionary streak surprises people, sometimes disorients and catches them off guard. It may be misunderstood but is always fascinating because it contains something different and original, and, above all, it reveals a perspective that no one had grasped.

Again, at times, their inability to understand the most banal, everyday matters can make things difficult for them; they understand others not for what might be said, but for what others might have wanted to say or should have said. Such sensitive and profound intelligence might even embarrass them, but then it is that very intelligence that knows how to be flexible, taking up the thread of the conversation when it seemed to have been lost.

Their mind, which functions with the laws of the heart, is always curious, it wants to grasp the impossible and unlimited, and wants to penetrate spiritual territories. While it may, occasionally, build castles in the air or lose itself in daydreams, or again seem hardly realistic and pass through moments of a certain degree of disorientation, in reality it always triggers a mental journey that brilliantly arrives at a precious truth in a world that is too caught up with banal calculations.

Sociability, Communication

and Friendship

Pisces has always been associated with meditation and spirituality, and therefore, with those moments of seclusion and silence in which the spirit finds itself again, ridding itself of the tension and clamor of the world. Pisces is also associated with forms of reclusiveness, even the enclosure and the peace of monasteries. The Pisces sensitivity and spiritual depth make it necessary for their character to be regularly removed from the chaos of the outside world. This is the reason why many of them need to disappear, isolate themselves from the many confused and confusing relations of 'normal' life. But, this does not mean that they are not sociable, quite the contrary.

In fact, their sociability is special precisely because it is not content with the mere forms and appearances of society life, fleeting but meaningless meetings, and all the superficiality based only on one's role and not on true self-awareness. Indeed, it is precisely their great capacity for empathy – which is sometimes really exaggerated and driven to feel others' problems too much – that leads them to immediately put themselves in contact with everything and everyone, and it may not be easy to sort things out in this huge flow of perception. Their feeling comes into play in the field of communication as well, making contact with others' hearts immediately and spontaneously.

On the one hand, this is a marvelous quality, because they instantly understand the person they are dealing with. But, on the other hand, this great empathy creates waves of uncontrolled emotion that sometimes ends up confusing and upsetting them. Consequently, they often feel the need to become invisible, even in the literal sense of this word, to disappear, while always remaining compassionate and altruistic.

In general, they do not like to speak loudly and emotionally, nor do they like to overwhelm others with a flood of words. They usually whisper, and their manner of speaking is never direct, but allusive. Their inconstant nature, their oscillation and moodiness, their lunar character that is sensitive to marked changes of mood, may disorient others who are arid and methodical and who consider friendship an obligation, while, for Pisces, being with others, speaking and listening, means absorbing their entire inner self, which often leads them to magnify the sense of what they say.

A phrase, a reference, a mere indication or hint trigger their oceanic imagination. Thus, while others are reasoning with them, they themselves have already, and instantly, made scores of connections, reflections and considerations. They are fluid, receptive, always ready to assimilate what others can teach them.

They may, occasionally, appear to be timid and some of them may even blush, but, ultimately, their passionate spirit comes to the fore. Despite the composed style of this spirit, its lack of impetus and vehemence, it is by no means cold and contemplative, but is inwardly agitated and immediately provides the solution to any problem it may be facing.

While they often seem to isolate themselves when they are in company, this is never due to indifference but stems from the fact that their exaggerated perception and highly intense feeling need to withdraw and have a short break.

In friendship also, there is the need for great affection, which is not only the desire to be heard when they lament the suffering and evil of the world, but is also their capacity and propensity for going immediately to someone's aid. Although they have a changeable, moody character, they never question friendship

When Pisces Gets Angry

Pisces is a lunar, passive, receptive sign. Rancor and hostility do not last long in Pisces. There is no pugnacity and violent anger in the Pisces character. Although there are dangerous Pisces tiger sharks, the peaceful, tranquil and contemplative side of their character often prevails, as it wants to be at peace with others. Rather than fearsome killer whales, they are cuttlefish who settle in the sand to beat a retreat from the racket of the world. However, there are matters that might transform their tender, innocuous sole into a barracuda. For example, questions of ideals and principles, because when they really believe in something they could easily become absolutists and, when faced with the injustice of the egoistic world, their utopian and decidedly bellicose side goes on the rampage.

Something else that might make them lose their patience is when someone wants to pigeonhole them in a particular category or too restrictive and specific a role, because they are the sign of the infinite and the broad horizons of the ocean, and being confined to narrow compartments, even those whose identity could be taken for granted, is absolutely not for Pisces.

Pisces is recalcitrant regarding rigid rules and regulations, or any milieu made up of timetables and social prisons. Anyone who wants to get along with them must not pester and plague them: having a gentle, courteous and compassionate nature certainly does not mean putting up with others' overbearing attitude. Whoever deals with them in some context or other must be aware that they are as innocent and poetic as a goldfish, but they are also as inexorable and razor-sharp as a swordfish.

A curious thing about their character is how they go about 'getting even'. They seem to suffer in silence, as they are paralyzed by anger, but then they use wholly unpredictable and imaginative 'battle tactics' that astonish and befuddle the other person.

Pisces
Children

The delicacy of the Pisces character, which verges on fragility, can be noted quite well in children born under the sign who, when they become adults, often generate a sense of protection for their helpless gentleness, for their insecure and absent-minded manner – although it must be said that these traits are often more appearance than substance. While Pisces children tend to be timid, anxious, in need of attention and confirmation, they are blessed with inner strength, resilience, and an uncanny capacity to react.

The young Pisces needs support and precise reference points, not so much because they are insecure (they know how to take care of themselves), but in order to have confirmation that they are right and have taken the right direction. Their parents must stand by them and impart a strong sense of protection and security, while at the same time leaving them free to have their own experiences. They must make their children feel sure that shelter will always be provided for them when needed. These children are imaginative and creative and love fairy tales, puppets, and games in which they can dress up. They tend to be impressionable, so it is best to keep them away from trauma, violent scenes and even frightening fables.

They are not always model pupils in school, since they tend to be distracted and do not study methodically. But if we stop to think that Einstein was born under Pisces, then it is clear that, for Pisces, distraction and wandering thoughts are synonymous with constant discovery and do not necessarily hinder the learning process.

At school, Pisces children do not distinguish themselves in any particular subject because they have an aptitude for mathematics as well as for music, poetry, and literature. Their natural inclinations will emerge during adolescence and then adulthood. Therefore, they should not be encouraged to follow a certain subject, but should be free to try different experiences, judge and choose the field in which they feel they will be most successful.

Music Associated

From the sparkling and passionate arias of Gioacchino Rossini to the dreamy and romantic melodies of Frédéric Chopin (for example, in his nocturnes), a lunar sign like Pisces is always quite comfortable with music; Pisces not only composes and plays music, but also listens to it for hours on end, as if a character like theirs was more in sync with the language of music than with that of cold, rational concepts. French composer Maurice Ravel (the author of the hypnotic and highly sensual *Boléro*) was also born under Pisces, as were the virtuoso Spanish guitarist Andrés Segovia, the violinist and composer Antonio Vivaldi, the great tenor Enrico Caruso, and the Russian composer Nikolaj Rimskij-Korsakov.

In popular and rock music, Pisces has given the world of music unforgettable and profound celebrities, from Lucio Dalla and Lucio Battisti to David Gilmour, one of the

with Pisces

ingenious and creative minds behind Pink Floyd. Gilmour's poetry immediately introduces us to those extraterrestrial worlds with which the Pisces nature has always been particularly intimate. The famous singer and pianist Nat King Cole was a Pisces, as was the rebellious and tragic Kurt Cobain. The ingenuity and eclectic nature of Pisces is also to be found in Jon Bon Jovi, singer/songwriter Erykah Badu, the irresistible Rihanna, the transgressive Johnny Cash and the poetic and essential Lou Reed. But, perhaps the atmosphere most compatible with Pisces in present-day rock music is the intense and meditative ambience created by Ry Cooder, especially in the soundtrack of the movie *Paris, Texas*. The instruments associated with Pisces are the harp, viola d'amore and especially the piano, with its vast range of expression.

Colors
Associated
with Pisces

Blue is the color Pisces, the color of the morning, of the sky we see when awakening, of the ocean's depths and the middle of the night. With blue, as with their imagination, there is room for everything, even for the clouds that eventually fade away, even for thoughts big or small that crop up and disappear like little darting fish. Blue like infinite space, which they need so much. Blue like the universe in which they float. It is a mystical and dreamlike color, like their nature. In ancient Egypt, it was the color of introspection and the infinite, a good luck charm for the afterlife. For the ancient Greeks and Romans blue was synonymous with diversity and danger because it was the color of barbarians, of foreigners. It is a relaxing color but is also disturbing, because in the blue of the night everything is indistinct, magical, and unfathomable. The glance dives into and loses itself in the blue of the sea or of the night, the mind opens out to consciousness as well as to the phantoms of vague and fuzzy thoughts. Like Pisces, this color is never boring since it promises mystery, infinite space, magical visions and deep introspection. Pisces should choose an inviting and receptive color such as ultramarine if they want to open out to the world, socialize, show others their most flexible and tender side. It is a hue that invites and provokes a smile and triggers their enterprising nature, which enjoys and experiences emotions rather than fleeing from them. It is the color of love, of falling in love and it enhances their fascination with a special light. Prussian blue is perfect for a work meeting because it makes them more open, empathetic, charismatic, and also more intelligent, astute and skilled in strategy. It is a hue of blue that helps them to act tactically and not only instinctively. For a sign like Pisces that attaches such importance to the signs of destiny, Persian blue sparks their intuition and raises their perceptive antennae. It is a tone that helps them to grasp and interpret the indications that life scatters and sows on one's path.

Flowers
and Plants
Associated
with Pisces

When the Sun is in Pisces, the wind brings new, fresh spring air. In the meadows the timid daisies, primroses and violets peep out, but it is flowers such as the periwinkle, alyssum, cineraria and daphne that are nearest to Pisces. The name of the last-mentioned flower (*daphnè* in Greek means 'laurel') refers to the aromatic plant that, together with the weeping willow, is closely associated with Pisces. For the ancient Greeks and Romans, the laurel symbolized glory and honor – a laurel wreath was worn on the heads of poets and triumphant athletes – but it was also considered a prophetic plant because the Pythia or the Oracle of Delphi chewed on laurel leaves before making prophecies. Pisces must rub laurel leaves in their hands if they must make an important decision or if they want a project to be successful. On the other hand, they must sit in front of a weeping willow if they want to ward off bad thoughts or find the strength to avoid being dominated or conditioned by anyone.

The following are the flowers and the plants for each 10-day period of Pisces.

First period (February 20-29): lily. Its elegance and fragrance epitomize their grace and capacity to enter into everyone's heart. This flower attracts attention and rewarding experiences to them, and in particular makes what they say more incisive and persuasive. If they carry the lily with them (either the flower or its essence) they will be able to communicate the incommunicable and make the indescribable describable.

Second period (March 1-10): Myosotis. Forget-me-not, this flower symbolizes the promise of love, the faithfulness and profundity of eternal love. This flower wards off anxieties of the heart.

Third period (March 11-20): cornflower. Cyanus segetum. Roman mythology has it that Flora, the goddess of flowers, loved fertility daemon Cyanus, who always dressed in blue. He died, and, out of love, Flora turned him into the flower. If Pisces places cornflower under a pillow, they have the power to talk, in their dreams, to those they love.

Animals Associated with Pisces

Pisces is the sign of oceanic Water, so that associated Pisces are marine and migratory birds, including the albatross, cormorant, heron, stork, wild goose, seagull, pelican and swallow. Some people accuse Pisces of being somewhat faint-hearted, of hiding their head in the sand like an ostrich, but this large bird is symbolically associated with Pisces because it runs in a zig zag fashion, much like their ability to move about with fluid dexterity in life.

Pisces is often symbolized by two fish swimming in opposite directions, which indicates the two Pisces types. There are friendly, insecure and emotional Pisces as well as resolute, combative, extroverted and very determined ones, tender goldfish as well as sharks. But, among all the marine animals, the dolphin is the one that best represents Pisces. Two dolphins saved Eros and Aphrodite from the fury of the monster Typhon; as a reward, Zeus placed them among the stars in the sky, thus giving rise to the Pisces constellation. For Pisces, the poetic and joyful dolphin expresses vivacious, scintillating movement in the world due to their vitality, which never stops or hesitates, which dives, disappears and reappears. Furthermore, the dolphin is one of the animals sacred to one of the rulers of Pisces, Neptune (Poseidon in ancient Greek mythology), the other being Jove (Zeus). The animals sacred to Neptune, the god of the sea, were the horse, bull and dolphin: the horse's crest is similar to sea foam, the bull's roar is likened to the sea during a storm, and the dolphin refers to the swiftness and elusiveness of water as well as the freedom to sail and swim in all seas.

There are also amphibians associated with Pisces: frogs, toads and newts. The word 'amphibian' comes from the Greek word *amphibios* or 'double life'. No other sign compares with Pisces in the ability to have a parallel existence, a double identity, and adopt a disguise, in a realm where a taste for adventure is combined with the need for escape.

Gemstones Associated with Pisces

The diamond, a symbol of purity, power and luminosity, is the gemstone corresponding to Pisces. The *Liber Lapidum* states that diamonds "will make you indomitable against your enemies, rivals and whoever performs evil acts, and will keep you safe from supercilious people. You will appear to be frightening to all men. This stone drives away all fear, all confused and idle dreams and the apparition of night spirits." Its hardness symbolizes the solidity of the Pisces character, which resists all pressure and tension. It is recommended that Pisces wear it to enhance the will, charisma, integrity and determination of their spirit. Diamonds also have a symbolic link with love, traditionally being mounted on engagement rings or given as a pledge of love. Its use for cutting – which in Tantric Buddhism symbolizes unalterable and invincible spiritual power – will help to end harmful relationships, love affairs in a state of breakdown that no longer bring joy to the heart, and situations that drive away peace. One legend has it that those who give diamonds to someone must do it with infinite love, otherwise their brilliance will slowly fade away. Another beneficial gemstone for Pisces is turquoise, with its characteristic greenish-blue color. It has been considered a precious stone since ancient times and in Central American cultures was associated with the god of fire or of the Sun. In his *Naturalis Historia*, Pliny the Elder wrote that turquoise "is attacked by oils, balsams and vice." This is a stone that radiates strength and will keep one away from dissipation and unhealthy, dangerous habits or company. For Pisces, ruled by Neptune, turquoise, if not used immoderately, imparts the strength to govern instincts, vices and weaknesses. Coral is also recommended. According to Greek mythology it was made of Medusa's blood, and, in antiquity, branches of coral were worn as amulets. This gift from the sea helps one overcome obstacles or, at the very least, find the simplest means to do so.

Best Food for Pisces

The analogy between Pisces and water suggests a diet particularly rich in liquids (tea, tisanes, fruit shakes and juices, and at least 1-2 quarts of water every day) and fruit like melons, watermelons, peaches and strawberries. Anatomically, Pisces is associated with the feet. This means that Pisces should not wear high-heeled shoes too much and not stand for a long time without moving about; it also calls their attention to the problem of water retention, which can be curbed through a diet rich in vitamin C that includes, among other things, citrus fruit, pineapple, kiwi, lettuce, radicchio, spinach, broccoli and potatoes.

Some say that Pisces are whiners but they can reply that, astrologically speaking, they are associated with tears, weeping, and emotional outbursts. Onions represent their tendency to produce tears easily and if they make them part of their diet they will have a food rich in vitamins and minerals. The ancient Egyptians associated the spherical shape of the onion with the concentric circles of eternal life. They also placed onions in their tombs because they believed its strong aroma would make the dead breathe again. Onions were also part of the diet of athletes in ancient Greece and of Roman gladiators. Besides enhancing food, onions have therapeutic properties; and they are a reminder - were this necessary - not to waste tears on those who do not deserve them.

The Jupiter side of Pisces delights in everything sweet and in a cereal, barley, which can be enjoyed in the form of bread, sweets and beer (barley coffee is also very good). As for spices, Pisces likes nutmeg, which has excellent antifungal, antioxidant, antidepressant and digestive properties, as well as dried fruit such as pistachio and almonds. Caviar, and fish such as anchovy, bass, trout and cod, are foods that are beneficial for Pisces.

Myths
Associated
with Pisces

Derceto was a mermaid goddess, depicted with the upper half of a woman, while the lower part was that of a fish. There are many legends about her. In one of these, Derceto became pregnant and was so ashamed she dove into the sea and died. Poseidon, the lord of the sea, was so angry at her suicide that he transformed her into a mermaid, and, thus, Derceto became the ancestor of mermaids.

Sirens, who beguiled sailors, and from whom Ulysses escaped, represent Pisces in mythological terms because they refer to their being torn between opposing emotions and sensations, between strength and fragility, passivity and action, the sense of life and the sense of death. However, this extraordinary changeability, the capacity to be something and its opposite, must not become insecurity, at times Pisces makes a mountain out of a molehill.

For those they love, they are the siren who bewitches, who suddenly appears, seduces and then disappears among the waves. Because they are quite skilled at vanishing, making others follow them, and disappearing if their partner becomes too predictable or they are bored with the relationship. They are a siren but they are also an undine, a water spirit. And like undines, they cross the oceans of life without ending up in any kind of net, because, for Pisces, freedom is everything.

Diana, the goddess of hunting, who loved solitude and hidden places, symbolizes the Pisces tendency to withdraw and isolate themselves. When the noises of the world become deafening they must find a warm refuge that is accessible them alone. They like solitude because it allows them to penetrate the silence of their soul. Diana was described as an irascible and vengeful goddess. This reminds us that, although Pisces is sweet and tender, it is not easy to convince or even force them to do something they don't want to do. They are fragile and delicate, but they also have great strength that is not easy to guide, coop up and subdue.

Pisces Fairy Tale

Love is everything for Pisces. Love is dreaming, the capacity to sacrifice oneself, to give everything of oneself. What can better describe the Pisces capacity to empathize with others, 'feel' them, than Hans Christian Andersen's *Little Mermaid*? The Little Mermaid was one of the daughters of the sea king. Her dreamy character led her to imagine what life must be like on land. At a one point, she was allowed to swim to the surface and rise up over the water, where she saw a ship and a very handsome prince, with whom she fell deeply in love. A terrible storm sank the ship and the Little Mermaid saved the prince, but she had to leave him on a beach, and since he was unconscious, there was no way he could see her. She was tormented by her great love for the prince, always sighing and in desperation. Finally, she went to ask for help from the Sea Witch, who, in exchange for the Mermaid's beautiful voice, gave her a magic potion that would change her fish tail into human legs. So, the Little Mermaid finally met the prince, but since she had no voice she could not talk to him! He was very affectionate to her, but this affection did not become true love. The Sea Witch had told her that if she did not succeed in marrying the prince she would die, so her sisters gave her a dagger; by killing the prince, she would save her own life and become a mermaid once again. But, the Little Mermaid could not kill the man she loved, so she threw herself into the sea and was transformed into white foam. The ocean and the open sea correspond to Pisces, but this fairy tale also represents Pisces because no one like Pisces is able to overcome distances, diversity, spatial and temporal barriers. The Little Mermaid also reminds us of the highly imaginative Pisces character. If Pisces were to stop dreaming then they would no longer be the same. They color the world with their imagination. But, they also have a practical side. They can rise up to the clouds, but when they come back down, they are full of practical ideas.

PATRIZIA TRONI, trained at the school of Marco Pesatori, writes the astrology columns for Italian magazines *Marie Claire* and *Telepiù*. She has worked in the most important astrology magazines (*Astra, Sirio, Astrella, Minima Astrologica*), she has edited and written the astrology supplement of *TV Sorrisi e Canzoni* and *Chi* for years, and she is an expert not only in contemporary astrology, but also in Arab and Renaissance astrology.

Photo Credits

Archivio White Star pages 28, 34, 38; artizarus/123RF page 20 center; Cihan Demirok/123RF pages 1, 2, 3, 4, 14, 30, 48; Yvette Fain/123RF page 46; file404/123RF page 16 bottom; Olexandr Kovernik/123RF page 42; Valerii Matviienko/123RF pages 8, 12; murphy81/Shutterstock page 44; Igor Nazarenko/123RF page 40; Michalis Panagiotidis/123RF pages 20, 21; tribalium123/123RF page 16; Maria Zaynullina/123RF page 36

vmb
PUBLISHERS

vmb Publishers® is a registered trademark property of De Agostini Libri S.p.A.

© 2015 De Agostini Libri S.p.A.
Via G. da Verrazano, 15 - 28100 Novara, Italy
www.whitestar.it · www.deagostini.it

Translation: Richard Pierce · Editing: Norman Gilligan

ISBN 978-88-540-2958-3
1 2 3 4 5 6   19 18 17 16 15

Printed in China